Symphony No. 5
in C Minor, Op. 67

Ludwig van Beethoven

DOVER PUBLICATIONS, INC.
Mineola, New York

Published in Canada by General Publishing Company, Ltd., 30 Lesmill Road, Don Mills, Toronto, Ontario.

Published in the United Kingdom by Constable and Company, Ltd., 3 The Lanchesters, 162–164 Fulham Palace Road, London W6 9ER.

Bibliographical Note

This Dover edition, first published in 1997, is a republication of music from *Symphonies de Beethoven. Partitions d'Orchestre,* originally published by Henry Litolff's Verlag, Braunschweig, n.d.

International Standard Book Number: 0-486-29850-7

Manufactured in the United States of America
Dover Publications, Inc., 31 East 2nd Street, Mineola, N.Y. 11501

CONTENTS

*Dedicated to Prince Franz Joseph von Lobkowitz
and Count Andrey Kyrilovich Razumovsky*

Symphony No. 5
in C Minor, Op. 67
(1807–8)

I. Allegro con brio   1

II. Andante con moto   17

III. Allegro   32

IV. Allegro   44

INSTRUMENTATION

Piccolo [Flauto piccolo, Fl. pic.]

2 Flutes [Flauti, Fl.]

2 Oboes [Oboi, Ob.]

2 Clarinets in C, B♭ ("B") [Clarinetti, Cl.]

2 Bassoons [Fagotti, Fag.]

Contrabassoon [Contrafagotto, C. Fag.]

2 Horns in C, E♭ ("Es") [Corni, Cor.]

2 Trumpets in C [Trombe, Tr.]

Alto Trombone [Tr. Alt(o)]

Tenor Trombone [Tr. Ten(ore)]

Bass Trombone [Tr. Bas(so)]

Timpani [Tp.]

Violins I, II [Violino]

Violas

Cellos & Basses [Violoncello,Vcl. & Basso]

Symphony No. 5
in C Minor, Op. 67

1

3

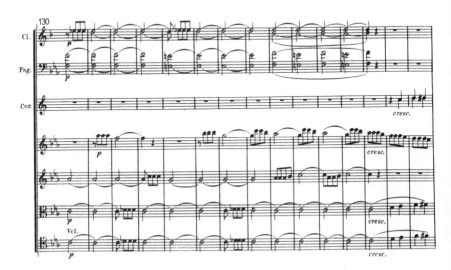

17

34

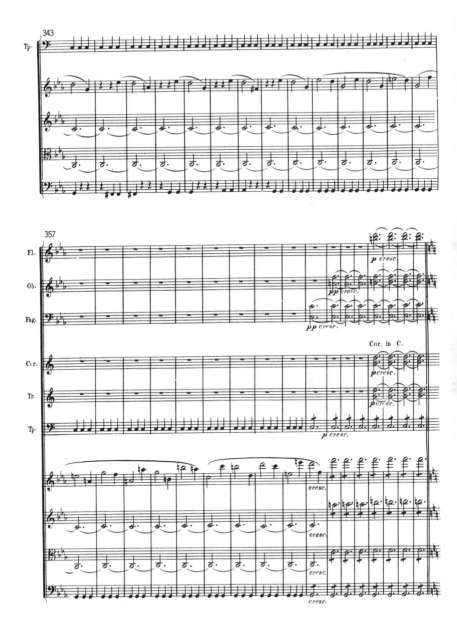

44

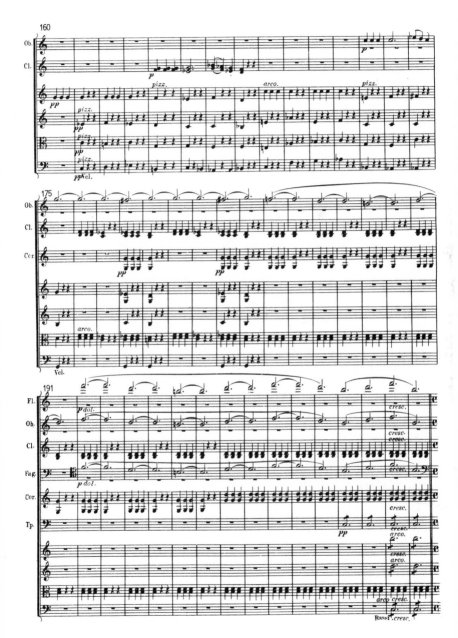

72

328

END OF EDITION